Cracking the Nut
on
Leadership
"A Way"

SAMUEL W. MORGAN, M.A.

Edited by: Christine DeGregory

Cover designed by: Michael Minas (redhawk@elp.rr.com)

Note for Librarians: a cataloguing record for this book that includes Dewey
Decimal Classification and US Library of Congress numbers is available from the
Library and Archives of Canada. The complete cataloguing record can be obtained
from their online database at:
www.collectionscanada.ca/amicus/index-e.html
ISBN 1-4120-5146-0
Printed in Victoria, BC, Canada

TRAFFORD

Offices in Canada, USA, Ireland, UK and Spain
This book was published *on-demand* in cooperation with Trafford Publishing.
On-demand publishing is a unique process and service of making a book available
for retail sale to the public taking advantage of on-demand manufacturing and
Internet marketing. On-demand publishing includes promotions, retail sales,
manufacturing, order fulfilment, accounting and collecting royalties on behalf of the
author.
Book sales for North America and international:
Trafford Publishing, 6E–2333 Government St.,
Victoria, BC v8t 4p4 CANADA
phone 250 383 6864 (toll-free 1 888 232 4444)
fax 250 383 6804; email to orders@trafford.com
Book sales in Europe:
Trafford Publishing (uk) Ltd., Enterprise House, Wistaston Road Business Centre,
Wistaston Road, Crewe, Cheshire cw2 7rp UNITED KINGDOM
phone 01270 251 396 (local rate 0845 230 9601)
facsimile 01270 254 983; orders.uk@trafford.com
Order online at:
www.trafford.com/robots/05-0041.html

10 9 8 7 6 5 4 3 2 1

Many of you apply some type of leadership in your daily endeavors but do not put much thought into how you achieve, or in many cases overcome, the challenging and complex tasks that you encounter and accomplish everyday. This book is designed to rekindle and generate thought about the importance of leadership in your personal, professional, and academic lives. Remember, you are not a leader just because you showed up.

CONTENTS

Dedication. vii
Introduction 1
What to Take Away From This Book 6
Why Concern Yourself with Leadership? 9
Myths and Beliefs 11
Defining Leadership? 19
Leadership: A Learned Process. 23
Positional and Emergent Leaders 26
Recipe for Leadership 33
The Educated Leader 46
The Irreversible Clock 50
Effective Communication 54
Technology's Impact 58
Effective Leadership 63
Balancing Personal Sacrifice with Collective Risk. . 67
Walking the Tightrope:Confidence vs. Arrogance . 72
Tyrannical Treatment 75
Providing Vision 78
Intangible Process – Quantifiable Product 84
Tomorrow's Leaders 87
Morgan's Tips for Success 93
What Do You Do Now? 95
About the Author 101

DEDICATION

"Be yourself, Samuel; you can't be anyone else."

—Bruce Alvin Bartholomew AKA "Bart"
1934-2000

This book is dedicated to my father, Bruce Alvin Bartholomew. He was my first and most influential mentor and the first person to teach me about the importance of leadership. It was through my father's dedication and perseverance in making sure I understood who I was as an individual and what I was capable of achieving, that

I gained a better understanding of myself, my limitations, my strengths, and the many other capabilities that I possess. He helped me to discover who Samuel Morgan was back then and who I have become today.

My father was one of the wisest men I have ever known. Although he was capable of telling me what I did well, he was also capable of telling me, in excruciating detail, at what I was failing. This candor and openness was not solely reserved for my pleasure, but for anyone in whom he had a vested interest. My father encouraged and supported me even when he did not agree with my decisions. He knew then, what I know today; that through education, experience, and time we can all develop the leadership skills that are required to make sensible and sound decisions in all aspects of our lives.

Although my father and I had many good times, we also had our fair share of bad ones. But through it all there was a respect that allowed us to communicate and move beyond our many differences. I could always count on my father to tell me the truth about how he perceived any situation. And regardless of his personal position, he could sympathize with whatever situation I was going through at the moment. It was his ability to "tell it like it is" and simultaneously comfort me that has permeated my very essence and has afforded me many opportunities to develop my leadership style over the years. In short, he never shied away from the hard issues, but rather he met them head on, as any true leader does.

My father displayed this type of personal courage consistently throughout his life. He taught me that the true test of your leadership ability is not when things are going well, but rather when things are going badly and in a hurry! Ultimately, your true leadership style is forged in how you deal with a situation during a crisis.

My father, until his dying day, never stopped encouraging me to develop and grow personally and professionally. He never stopped believing in me—even when I did not believe in myself. And so this is to whom I dedicate this book. Dad, thank you! You will always be my greatest source of inspiration. You are truly missed.

INTRODUCTION

"A most important key to successful leadership is your ability to direct and challenge the very best that is in those whom you lead."

—Unknown Author

Many people are intrigued with the topic of leadership. After all, everyone and everything on this planet is impacted by what leaders or so-called leaders consistently do or fail to do. On any given day, there are countless numbers of people who are searching for information on how they, too, can become effective leaders. They are hoping to gain a better understanding of what leadership is and how it can be used to assist them in attaining their personal, professional, and academic goals. At this point, it would be safe to assume that those of you reading this

1

book fit into this "searching" category. In your efforts to better understand leadership, you have found this book. Whether you are just starting out or are a more seasoned leader, this book will assist you in developing and refining your leadership skills to their fullest potential.

Cracking the Nut on Leadership will also provide you with tools to aid you in your quest to become a more effective and productive leader. Everyone, regardless of their economic, educational, or social status has some unrealized leadership potential. This potential can be developed over time, but only if an individual has a sincere desire to influence the actions of others. It saddens me greatly that often the leadership potential, which an individual possesses, will remain unrealized without some type of intervention by an outside force or a significant level of self-awareness. For most, this self-awareness and intervention will only materialize during a personal crisis or a significant, emotional event in an individual's life.

To effectively wield leadership it is necessary to personally discover and understand what leadership is and what effects leadership has on individuals, teams, groups, societies, and the world. Developing your leadership ability starts with a sincere personal desire to lead others. Next, you must improve upon your self-awareness and have a firm understanding of your environment (personal, professional, and academic) coupled with an honest assessment of your personal abilities (strengths and weaknesses). All of this must be achieved in order to transform yourself from your current status to where you really want to be: a practitioner of effective leadership in the future. An honest assessment of your personal strengths and weaknesses is by far the most difficult task you will have to perform in your quest to become an effective leader. It is this personal struggle of being honest with one's self that provides the building blocks in establishing a solid leadership foundation. Sometimes the truth hurts. However, in many instances, the truth is less stressful and less painful than the false self-image many so-called leaders have of themselves with regards to their true abilities and potential. If you do not acknowledge your weaknesses, you will never fully realize your leadership potential.

It has been my experience that those who do not know how to lead, but nevertheless occupy leadership positions, tend to do what they "think" they are supposed to do as a leader instead of actually becoming a leader. In other words, they pretend to lead, or even worse, they make it up as they go along. These "spotlight" individuals seem to only utilize their "leadership abilities" when they are in direct observation by their leaders. If these so-called leaders were honest with themselves, they would not subject their teams, groups, or organizations to their ineffective leadership. The perception of reality that these so-called leaders try to convince themselves of hurts the entire organization in the long run. Remember, you can lie to your friends, you can lie to your family, you can even lie to me, but you can never lie to yourself. Instinctively, we know what we are capable of doing just as we inherently know right from wrong. Nonetheless, the truth eludes many people. Instead of basing their end goals upon an honest assessment of their personal, professional, and academic abilities and competencies, they base them on a false or unrealistic sense of self. Many so-called leaders would like to be the best in their field, but few, if any of these individuals, possess the personal initiative, discipline, commitment, and skills required to achieve such a notable status.

Regardless of your position in life, you can develop your leadership ability if you have a sincere desire to lead others. You must realize that true leadership is not a process that can be achieved over night; however, through education, experience, and time you can develop the necessary mindset and skills required to successfully lead teams, groups, and organizations. Together we will attempt to "crack the nut on leadership" and discover what leadership is and how effective leadership can be applied in your daily life in an effort for you to become a more effective leader in all that you do. At a minimum, my thoughts and experiences will provide you with "a way" of thinking about the development and application of your leadership abilities today and in the future. Through effective leadership, leaders make us believe in the impossible. Dare to dream!

WHAT TO TAKE AWAY FROM THIS BOOK

"Leadership makes all the difference!"

—Major General Michael A. Vane
Commanding General, United States Army
Air Defense Artillery Center, Fort Bliss, Texas

This book is designed to offer the reader with a perspective on effective leadership. It will also provide the reader with a better understanding of the dynamics associated with applying leadership on a daily basis. Leadership is not reserved for the few. When given the proper tools, anyone can be capable of exercising leadership at any level of an organization under any circumstance. The ability to exercise this leadership is how organizations develop, grow, and integrate their future leaders.

Effective leadership will also assist you in better

preparing yourself, your followers, and your organization for the many difficult challenges that you will face today and in your future endeavors. Through a basic understanding of the concepts associated with leadership, you will be better able to visualize, anticipate, and mitigate many of the obstacles that would otherwise impede your ability to influence the actions of others.

True leaders apply leadership on a regular and consistent basis, and they recognize that leadership development is a never-ending process. They also understand the second, third, and fourth order effects of their decisions on followers and their organization as a whole. Therefore, true leaders will always attempt to ensure that the proverbial i's are dotted and t's are crossed before making decisions that will impact the lives of every person and everything within their sphere of influence.

Three questions you will be able to answer after reading this book are:

- **Why is leadership important?**
- **What are the characteristics of an effective leader?**
- **Who should be concerned about leadership?**

In answering these questions you will be well on your way to success in any endeavor you undertake in life.

This book was not written to convince you that I have the best method of developing and applying leadership. Rather it is "a way" for me to convey my thoughts on the importance of leadership, and if properly applied, how effective leadership is the crux of any successful individual or organization. Dare to challenge the status quo!

WHY CONCERN YOURSELF WITH LEADERSHIP?

"In order to succeed, you must know what you are doing, like what you are doing, and believe in what you are doing."

—Will Rogers
American Humorist, Actor, and Writer

The practice of leadership is timeless. There have always been men and women who have assumed the mantle of leadership to lead others in building great societies, nations, and empires. Leaders provide purpose, direction, motivation, and the resources needed to attain the goals and objectives of a team, group, or organization. Leadership is a real and powerful force. After all, our quality of life can be impacted positively or negatively, by what our leaders do or fail to do. Sadly, this is an idea we often dismiss. Leadership is an awesome responsibility that should not be taken for granted; therefore, individuals need to be more aware of how someone else's influence affects their lives and the world.

The leadership process impacts the lives of every person on the planet by playing a role in situations involving environmental issues, social programs, education, local and world economies, basic human rights, and governments. Leadership should not be approached from the standpoint of out of sight, out of mind. Therefore, it is my sincere desire to educate others on the topic of leadership.

MYTHS AND BELIEFS

"You manage things; you lead people."

—Grace Murray Hopper
U.S. Navy Admiral and Computer Scientist

There are a myriad of myths and beliefs about leadership that others would like for you to believe. Listed below are some of these myths and beliefs:

- Leaders are born
- Leaders are perfect (they do no wrong)
- Leaders are always formally designated
- Leaders know everything (they have all the answers)
- Leaders look like leaders
- Management and leadership are one in the same

· Academic accomplishment equates to leadership ability.

· All leaders are ethical

In my opinion, none of these statements are true. They are myths much like the Loch Ness Monster or Bigfoot. It seems that these leadership myths were created, fostered, and perpetuated by those in positions of power. These myths are a means of deterring others from attempting to move into positions of authority; thereby keeping current leaders in charge. To those of you that believe these myths, it must seem to you that the leaders of many organizations somehow appear to be larger than life. Perhaps it is even a bit comforting for you to believe so.

One myth that has truly taken over many mindsets is that there is no distinction between managers and leaders. I completely disagree with this. Management and leadership have differing goals. Management's primary focus, as it should be, is to maintain systems and the status quo – planning, staffing, organizing, and controlling. Managers are concerned with efficiency. The purpose of management is to control and mitigate any chaos that may arise in an organization. Leadership, on the other hand, is about people. Leaders, through their constant analysis and desire to improve, focus on constructive change that will move teams, groups, and organizations forward to achieve the organization's goals and objectives. Leaders are concerned about both effectiveness and efficiency.

Although there is much overlap between management and leadership in their attempts to make an organization successful, there are also some fundamental differences that set the two apart. Leaders have vision and provide the inspiration and motivation for organizations to move in new directions. Managers maintain the status quo by providing stability and restraint. Leaders are proactive; managers are reactive. It is one thing to know of principles and concepts, but it is an entirely different thing to understand and be capable of implementing them. It seems to me that leaders are the visionaries who see the bigger picture. A manager never thinks about taking an organization to the next level. A leader would examine an organization and be able to envision the changes necessary to make it better.

Another common myth surrounding the topic of

leadership is that of ethics. Does a leader have to be ethical in their dealings with others to be considered a leader? Everyone on the planet, foregoing a rare exceptional few, wants to be a part of something larger than themselves. I would contend that under the right circumstances even the most unlikely and unsavory individuals can become leaders in their own right. History is full of such individuals who have led and influenced the actions of entire nations and groups of people. Adolf Hitler, Jim Jones, and Pablo Escobar are but a few who understood the power of leadership and influenced hundreds, even thousands, of followers to do their bidding.

Many people have adopted the school of thought that all leaders are ethical. I disagree with this notion. Regardless of their ethos, or lack thereof, people who have the ability to influence others to work towards their ultimate goal or objective, are in fact, exercising leadership. It seems to me that some of the above mentioned individuals had many leadership qualities and thus were able to influence others to work towards their vision, as unethical or self-serving as they may have been.

· **Adolf Hitler:** Though Austrian-born, he rose to

power in Germany during the 1920s and early 1930s at a time of social, political, and economic upheaval. Failing to take power by force in 1923, he eventually won power by democratic means. Once in power, he eliminated all opposition and launched an ambitious program of world domination and elimination of the Jews.

· **Jim Jones:** Despite being a sociopath, one must marvel at the level of loyalty he achieved and his people skills. First, he transformed his mainstream San Francisco congregation into a full-blown religious cult. Next, he convinced the government of Guyana to give him 300 acres of South American jungle and relocated 1,100 cult members to this distant site. Finally, in 1978 Jones still managed to convince 900 followers to swallow poison in a massive suicide, the likes of which the world had never seen.

· **Pablo Escobar:** Escobar's rise to power began as a small-time gangster to the terror of Colombia. He was arguably the richest and most violent criminal in history. *Forbes* magazine in 1989 listed him as the seventh-richest man in the world.

Even madmen have been looked to for leadership by their followers. Although this is not a popular line of reasoning, the fact remains that no one has rivaled what these three have accomplished since their necessary fall. These madmen embodied and displayed leadership and had the ability to influence the actions of their followers to achieve their individual or organizational goals and objectives.

What we can learn from history is that there are leaders who inspire people to do great and just deeds (Martin Luther King Jr., Gandhi, John F. Kennedy, etc.), as well as leaders who inspire people to do great evil (Hitler, Jones, Escobar, etc.). These leaders could not have been more different in their beliefs and ideology; however, the fact remains that they all had the ability to influence individuals and groups of individuals, thereby moving entire nations and empires towards their goals and objectives. All of these leaders were capable of conveying their vision so clearly that their followers not only bought into it but in some cases made the ultimate sacrifice for them. They were so influenced that they laid down their very lives for their leaders. Would you be willing to die for what someone else believes in?

Someone once told me that it would be impossible to convince an individual to do something if that individual's values were not in keeping with what was being asked of them. If this were a true statement, there would be no amount of money, glory, fame, or fear that could be used to persuade an individual to go against their beliefs. However, we know that these things do influence people in their decision-making as seen by leaders who make promises of them. The fact is that we are all greatly influenced by the leaders around us.

In the end, does leadership have to follow a perceived notion or societal norms to truly be considered leadership? The answer to this question might help you to understand how effective leadership permits individuals to influence the actions of others positively and negatively. I believe that the influence, which has been wielded by the likes of

Hitler, Jones, and Escobar, albeit evil, is in fact leadership and effective leadership at that.

DEFINING LEADERSHIP?

"When you know better, you do better."

—Oprah Winfrey
Philanthropist, Owner-HARPO Productions,
Entertainment Executive, and Entrepreneur

I would be remiss, if not deceitful, if I did not clearly state to you that there is no simple answer or single definition that can fully encapsulate the meaning of leadership. At best, defining leadership is an arduous task. One never gives good leadership a second thought; you just know it, when you experience it.

The development of an individual's leadership ability is a process; leadership involves the ability to consistently influence the actions of individuals or groups of individuals towards a goal or objective. Leadership requires

that leaders be capable of influencing the actions of
other people. Leadership is all about people. Leadership
does not exist if leaders are incapable of influencing the
actions of others to achieve goals and objectives. Based
on this basic understanding of leadership, the following
definition will be used throughout this book: **"Leadership is the process of consistently influencing other
individuals toward the achievement of some goal or
objective."**

There are countless definitions of leadership used
throughout society. A single definition or style of leadership will not and cannot fit everyone's needs or every
situation. There are no cookie cutter solutions to the
development and application of leadership. Simply put,
what works for me might not necessarily work for you
and vise versa. As you will see in a later section, this does
not mean that leadership is not quantifiable, but rather
that your true leadership ability is grounded in your
knowledge of yourself, your knowledge of your followers
or potential followers, and your knowledge of your
environment. People and situations change and so must
your approach to leadership as you lead teams, groups,

and organizations. To be successful in leading you must be flexible and adaptable in your approach. You must be capable of identifying what needs to be accomplished; understand the current situation and be on the lookout for future difficulties or opportunities; and know the abilities of your followers and the skill sets required to achieve your goals or objectives.

Leadership has been a subject that has long fascinated scholars and laypeople alike. The subject of leadership has captured the imagination of us all at one time or another. As many of you may have already come to realize, leadership is a slippery concept to nail down. But through your self-awareness, awareness of your environment, and a basic understanding of leadership, it should not seem all that elusive to you any longer. When it comes to understanding leadership, I do not claim to have all of the answers. I will, however, provide you with a starting point from which you can begin to understand for yourself what leadership is and is not.

So how does one influence others towards achievement of goals and objectives? First, leadership is about people and how they interact with one another and their environment. From my experience, some of the leaders within industries, the government, and society lose sight and fail to realize that every organization, regardless of how large or how small, is dependant on and utilizes the same precious resource–people. Individuals are the single most important resource that can make an organization topnotch. An organization can produce the best products and services, but it is ultimately the people who perform the day-to-day functions that set one organization apart from another.

Today, more than any time in history, organizations need to focus their efforts and resources on developing the leadership potential of the individuals that make up the organization. Organizations that focus their efforts on leadership development of their followers will reap the benefits of their labor through higher retention of qualified personnel, lower turnover at all levels, and improved productivity. This exercise of leadership and the development of junior leaders demonstrates how consistently influencing other individuals results in the achievement of a goal or objective.

LEADERSHIP: A LEARNED PROCESS

"There is only one thing more painful than learning from experience, and that is not learning from experience."

—Archibald McLeish
American Poet and Critic

Most of our society tends to believe that leaders are born. Others think leadership is something that can be developed in everyone. And then there are those that believe leadership is reserved for the economically and academically privileged.

True leadership is a process that takes time to develop. The development of an individual's leadership ability doesn't happen overnight. Leaders must possess an extensive repertoire of skills that are relevant to what the leader does, as well as, what the leader might have to do in the future. If an individual has a sincere desire to lead other people, the skills that are required of a leader can be acquired and improved upon over time.

To truly understand the magnitude and the impact that leadership has on our everyday lives, you must first set aside your preconceived notions of what you believe leadership is. In an effort to fully understand how true leadership is exercised by others and how this leadership impacts the lives of every person on this planet, you must be able to approach the leadership development process with an open mind.

It is my sincere belief that leadership is a learned process. Everything a person is and everything that a person will become is the sum total of every situation and experience an individual has encountered over the course of their lifetime. No one awakens to discover that they are suddenly a great leader capable of leading and influencing other men and women. From the cradle to the grave, your leadership skills can be developed and improved upon if you are aware enough to know that you have leadership potential inside of you. The individual leadership development process only ends at death. True leaders have the capacity to influence others until their dying breath and beyond. Think about it!

POSITIONAL AND EMERGENT LEADERS

"No man will make a great leader who wants to do it all himself, or to get all the credit for doing it."

—Andrew Carnegie
U.S. Steel Manufacturer, Philanthropist

Some believe leaders are born, others believe leaders are made. Some believe leaders are chosen by their followers, and others believe that leaders are simply people who seize the opportunity to lead. I believe there are two main sources of leadership, positional and emergent leaders. These two sources of leadership are easily identified in most organizations. Positional leaders are the formally designated, acknowledged, and titled leaders within teams, groups, and organizations. The second source of leadership is an emergent leader and is not necessarily

26

recognized by the formal organization. This source of leadership is dependant upon what an individual does and how their followers perceive their ability to lead.

Being assigned as a positional leader does not guarantee that an individual will be an effective leader; in many instances they are not. It only formally designates them as a leader. The positional leader must prove their ability to lead others towards the attainment of the goals and objectives of the organization. However, positional leaders have to prove themselves more so to their followers, rather than to their leaders, who appointed them to their position in the first place. Examples of positional leadership based on formality can be executives, directors, administrators, and military leaders.

Emergent leadership is based on the perceived abilities an individual has by their peers, leaders, and followers. An emergent leader can be someone who has a considerable amount of influence over the members of a team, group, or organization. Regardless of title or formal position within an organization, the emergent leader can assume a leadership role within it. This source of leadership relies heavily upon what an individual does and how their followers perceive their ability as a leader. In many cases, the emergent leaders within organizations are considered to be subject matter experts. They are your go-to people; the individuals that you know you can count on to achieve results. This type of leadership is not formal in nature, but emerges over a period of time.

Emergent leaders are active in achieving the goals and objectives of the organization. They are visible in the daily activity of the organization and take initiative by making things happen. Typically, emergent leaders can be more influential than positional leaders. Emergent leadership is a powerful resource in countless organizations.

Despite whether an individual is a positional leader or an emergent leader, that individual is engaged in the leadership process. Those who believe their source of leadership and influence comes from their position within an organization are misguided in their beliefs. In my opinion, this assumption could not be further from the truth. An individual's ability to effectively exercise leadership and consistently influence the actions of others comes not from position but rather from the trust, respect, and actual or perceived competence of a leader by their followers. Leaders must, above all else, establish a mutual trust with their followers. This trust can be fostered through a shared sense of purpose derived from the common vision driving the organization. Trust is critical to any leader who ever hopes to achieve their vision.

Leadership that is exhibited by true leaders is comprised of many complex components. Consider this, if a person in a leadership position does not exercise their leadership abilities, regardless of the position that they hold within an organization, in essence no leadership has been asserted or exercised at all. Many of you probably know someone who occupies a leadership position, but their effectiveness as a leader is at best limited, if not nonexistent. The individuals in these leadership positions are not leaders, but rather figureheads since they do not rise to the occasion and effectively influence their followers on a regular and consistent basis. If you were to look behind-the-scenes of many of these "figurehead" organizations, you would find at least one or two emergent leaders who are responsible for the actual influence and change taking place within the organization.

Unfortunately, poor leadership is perpetuated within many organizations due to customs, courtesies, myths, and bureaucracy regarding organizational leadership. There is a need for a fundamental change in paradigms with respect to leadership practices. A better understanding of leadership is desperately needed to prevent much of the nonsense that is being passed off and accepted as leadership in our schools, churches, government, and society. Becoming a leader is a demanding and difficult process. It is even more difficult to remain a leader if the leader does not understand and accept all of the ramifications of their decisions and behaviors while executing their leadership responsibilities.

There will be many obstacles impeding the path of your leadership development process, but do not allow this to discourage you in your leadership quest. A poem that has always given me the ability to persevere through the hard times is entitled "Don't Quit" by an unknown author:

"Don't Quit"

When things go wrong, as they sometimes will,

When the road you're trudging seems all uphill,

When the funds are low, and the debts are high,

And you want to smile but you have to sigh,

When care is pressing you down a bit,

Rest if you must but don't you quit.

Life is queer with it's twists and turns,

As every one of us sometimes learns,

And many a failure turns about,

When you might have won had you stuck it out.

Don't give up though the pace seems slow,

You may succeed with another blow.

Success is failure turned inside out,

The silver tint of the clouds of doubt,

And you never can tell how close you are,

It may be near when it seems so far,

So stick to the fight when you're hardest hit,

It's when things seem worst,

That you must not quit.

RECIPE FOR LEADERSHIP

"It is very easy to develop an effective leadership style if you are a good follower."

—Charles E. Ellis
Deputy United States Marshal and Major,
United States Marine Corps Reserve

Everything that you currently know you learned through a process. Someone who possessed an understanding of what you needed to know taught you what was necessary in order for you to function or survive in your environment. In essence, you have been conditioned by the system to believe, think, and interact with others through a process known as socialization or social conditioning. I once read that "conformity is a social disease." As a society we tend to conform to what we have learned from others and leadership plays an essential role in this learning.

Becoming a leader is not an easy process. Just ask someone who has dedicated his or her life to a social cause that others do not believe in as strongly as they do. The ability to keep people inspired and moving forward in the face of adversity requires leaders of character who remain steadfastly committed to their role as a leader. Leaders must also possess competence, initiative, respect, and loyalty in an effort to influence their followers.

Why do certain leaders elicit such a loyal following, whereas others do not? Why does one style of leadership work in one situation, but fails in another? Leadership is a more complex matter than just having someone occupy a position and calling them a leader. It takes the ability of the leader to comprehend and understand the bigger picture and be able to thoroughly articulate that vision to others in an effort to have them follow you. The process by which leaders are made is rooted in this ability to take information with which you are unfamiliar and utilize it to formulate a response or to take action.

The process of developing leadership begins with an

understanding of yourself and continues each day of your life. Your strengths and weaknesses as a leader need to be clearly identified. A technique that has served me well has been to periodically jot down what I consider to be my strengths and weaknesses in a notebook. Once I have conducted my self-assessment I query others who know me either personally or professionally for their assessments of my strengths and weaknesses. Be sure to insist that the individuals you ask give you honest feedback. Many individuals have been so conditioned by the system they will sugarcoat their response for fear of hurting your feelings. Assure them that your feelings will not be hurt, since it was you who approached them for that feedback, not the other way around.

Once you receive this treasured information, consolidate your two lists of strengths and weaknesses. Review the lists for duplications and highlight them. This will give you a good sense of what you and others perceive as your strengths and weaknesses. By cross-referencing in this manner you will narrow your focus in the area of personal strengths and weaknesses. Any strengths and weaknesses that you did not identify, but others have identified, will give you more insight as to how others perceive your leadership ability.

Next, prioritize your list and identify how you are going to sustain your strengths while determining how you will improve upon your weaknesses. You might have noticed that I said improve upon, not compensate for your weaknesses. If you continue to compensate by hiding from or avoiding situations that require you to act in your weak areas, you will never be able to turn your weaknesses into strengths.

I am a strong advocate that weaknesses are areas that you need to focus on and change within yourself. If there is an area where I perceive myself to be weak, I purposely place myself in situations where I have no choice but to increase my competency in an effort to avoid future embarrassment. This is a technique that I have utilized to develop my personal assets and I recommend that you should practice as well.

It is one thing to know what to do, but it is another to do the right thing. True leadership is all about choosing the harder right over the easier wrong. Leaders say what they mean and mean what they say. They possess the ability to do the right thing, even if it is not popular with the masses. Trust is a by-product of a leader's integrity. Trustworthiness is a must if a leader aspires to be an effective leader of other people and organizations. The leader must be capable of garnering the trust of their followers, for it is the leader's followers that give trust. I have found that if followers within an organization trust their leaders, they will be more productive and more efficient in performing their duties and responsibilities. Of course, this does not mean that leaders are perfect—no one is! But true leaders learn from their mistakes and continue to move forward, never dwelling too long on the past.

If you have followers that are not capable of doing the right thing even with proper education, training, and when clear guidance has been given, it is your sacred responsibility as a leader to dismiss that person from their duties by sending them on their way! As General Bernard W. Rogers once said, "This [the Army] is a volunteer force, and soldiers volunteer to meet our standards. If they don't meet them, we should thank them for trying and send them home." The same goes for leaders.

To fire or relieve another person of their duties is not easy, but it is necessary in organizations that depend on the efforts of others to ensure the future survival of the organization.

One never gives good leadership a second thought. It is transparent and everyone within the organization benefits from it. On the other hand, poor or bad leadership adversely affects the entire organization and everyone within the organization suffers from the consequences. Ineffective leaders should be removed and replaced by those who are willing to put the time and effort into the responsibility of the leadership position.

Another benefit a leader can provide their organization with is setting and adhering to standards. It has been my experience that many so-called leaders do not hold their followers accountable for adhering to organizational standards, thereby establishing a new "lower standard." If there are no consequences associated with poor performance or misconduct by their followers, followers will continue their negative behavior. If leaders do not correct the inappropriate behavior of their followers then the leaders will have to deal with the consequences of their inactions.

If leaders are not holding their followers to the set standard, there would be no reason to have standards in the first place. By holding your followers accountable for meeting minimum standards, they will rise to the challenge of meeting or exceeding any standard established for them. Furthermore, even if only one member of an organization is not held to the standard, others in the organization will see that their efforts to meet or exceed the standards are diminished or unnecessary. Meeting standards will instill discipline, a sense of pride, and a sense of accomplishment in your followers. As Brigadier General Abraham J. Turner once told me, "Hold them [followers] accountable, standards are everything." This is very true for leadership, as the standards set by the leader create the atmosphere for the organization. This idea is reiterated in Command Sergeant Major Phillip Rowland's statement, "Be brutally honest with your soldiers [followers]. Ensure that they know that you expect more from them than the status quo. Insist that they go beyond what is expected of them; hold them accountable for thinking through situations."

Just as you expect your followers to be aware of their actions, it should be acknowledged that followers are observing your every action as a leader. Most followers watch you to see what right looks like. Consequently, ineffective leadership culminates in ineffective future leaders throughout the organization. I have been quoted on many occasions as saying to my students, peers, and colleagues that the most dangerous thing to an individual's existence is to be observed and not know that you are being observed. Understand that everything you do speaks volumes about who you are and what your organization represents.

Another part of the process of becoming an effective leader is determining who is in your span of influence and how you can utilize their varied skill sets to effectively disseminate your vision to the entire organization. For example, a Company Commander (organizational leader) in the United States Army has essentially eight followers within their span of influence that they can utilize to effectively lead the entire organization (120+

personnel). These followers include one Executive Officer, three Platoon Leaders, one First Sergeant, and three Platoon Sergeants. It is through these eight junior leaders that the Company Commander can expand their vision to the entire company by effectively directing the eight to influence the rest.

Understanding your span of influence is an essential tool for effective leadership. Yes, you, as the leader, are overall responsible for everyone and everything within your organization. But don't forget that you have leaders and followers in your span of influence that are receiving a paycheck thereby allowing you to focus on the bigger picture for your organization. If you allow others within your organization to carry out their duties and responsibilities, you will find it easier to provide an accurate assessment of the potential and abilities of the future leaders you are developing within your organization.

As a leader, you will inevitably see the adage of the "cream always rises to the top" come to life. The flipside of this is that the duds will always sink. This process will allow you to properly reward competency and release those that are collecting a paycheck that they have not truly earned. This method can only be effective if you have properly screened applicants, educated and trained them to standard, and given them proper guidance in their duties and responsibilities. Just as babies learn, developing leaders must crawl before they walk and walk before they run. This is a process that must be adhered to in order to be successful. Unfortunately, many organizations fail to properly teach, coach, and mentor their followers.

Jumping in and getting one's feet wet is much easier for an individual if they know in advance what they are jumping into. It is in the best interest of an organization to develop an initiative-oriented follower group. By pursuing this mindset, a true understanding of this Chinese Proverb can be understood. "Tell me and I will forget; show me and I may remember; involve me and I will understand." Allow your followers to make mistakes without ending their careers; in other words, be understanding of honest mistakes. Provide them plenty of opportunity to hone their leadership potential and continue to develop their abilities. This is how effective leadership is applied. Remember, no one is perfect!

To be an effective leader, you must have the capacity to think outside of the box. Curiosity plays a large role in a leader's ability to do so. Being curious helps the leader in the formulation of appropriate questions that need answering in an effort to get past the obvious and dig below the surface to get at the root cause of all issues, not just the superficial ones. In doing so a leader gains a better understanding of situations that affect their followers, their organizations, and themselves.

Curiosity is a very important component of the leadership development process and is a great source of creativeness for most leaders. This is what sets successful organizations apart from other organizations that are merely existing and surviving. Curiosity also provokes thought. Curiosity encourages risk taking. Curiosity is a must to ensure that leaders and followers continue to bring fresh new ideas to their teams, groups, and organizations. If leaders are not curious about the issues, situations, and the people around them, there is a very good chance that they will never influence anyone or any situation in a meaningful manner.

Leadership also demands that individuals have some

identifiable competence, that they are committed to what they are doing, and that they possess the necessary skills to perform what is expected of them as a leader. If you are missing competence, commitment, and skills, then you're probably not the right person to lead other people.

The ability to think critically helps leaders to go beyond the obvious. The status quo is not good enough for a true leader. In other words, leaders are capable of thinking through situations critically while keeping the big picture or overarching purpose of the team, group, or organization in mind. Leaders make decisions based on fact, as well as on assumptions. This ability to make decisions is based on the leader's education and experiences. They also have an intuitive ability to see things that others are incapable of or unwilling to see. Leaders do not wait to be told what to do, rather they possess the instinct and personal courage to make decisions and take action when situations dictate.

It is not uncommon for leaders to perform a sort of mental gymnastics in an effort to tie concepts and theory to the reality of a situation, while all the time remaining firmly grounded in the practical application of how business is really conducted within their particular industry. Digging below the surface is not having the ability to recite verbatim the policy, regulation, or procedure, but rather it is the capacity of a leader to think critically about a given issue or situation and go beyond the status quo if it is necessary. It is not enough to do the minimum that is required to perform one's duties, but going the extra distance to ensure that it is done correctly and to an acceptable standard of measure is, in fact, the right answer. True leaders take the initiative, not only to do what is required of them, but they go one further and do what needs to be done without being told or reminded about it.

Finally, if the leadership development process is conducted effectively, as senior leadership moves on to new challenges, there will be a follower or two who is ready to assume this recently vacated leadership position. True leaders instill initiative in all of their followers' actions, but more importantly produce thinking organizations capable of taking proper action in the absence of formally designated leadership.

THE EDUCATED LEADER

"Education is the mother of leadership."

—Wendell Lewis Willkie
American Industrialist and
1940 Republican Presidential Candidate

Education is a major contributor to the leadership development process. Every person has been shaped or molded in some facet by their environment; we are the sum total of all of our experiences. Everything learned happens through a process of trial and error. Life's educational process molds and shapes us into the leaders we are today and the leaders we will be tomorrow. Everything we know and everything we will ever know is a learned process that can be built upon. Just about everyone has the capability to learn how to become an effective leader.

To what degree this takes place will depend upon one's cognitive abilities and one's personal desire to be an effective leader.

The education that helps create an effective leader can be formal or informal in nature. Most leaders intuitively know what they know and possess a clear understanding of what they do not know. Therefore, they undertake a journey or quest in the pursuit of attaining an education that will assist them in achieving their goals. An investment in your education today, is an investment in your future. Leaders are lifelong learners who understand that when we stop learning, we stop growing and developing as a person, citizen, and leader. A solid education is the bedrock upon which your leadership abilities are continually developed.

True leaders understand the need for formalized education in their developmental process but also value the informal education they have received. True leaders realize that the knowledge and skills gained through the formalized educational process can provide them with some very real and necessary tools, but understand that alone it does not make them a leader. A true leader must also be a lifelong learner. They realize that they are never too old to learn something new. It also means being open to new ideas, being trustworthy, being respectful of others, to admit when you're wrong, and possessing the personal courage to stand by your convictions even if others do not agree.

Mentorship is an excellent way of attaining knowledge in an informal manner. Mentors will help you in your quest to develop your leadership abilities by sharing their experiences. Mentorship also provides the individuals being mentored with the opportunity to establish contacts that they would otherwise not have access to on their own. What I mean by contacts is not meeting people so to network your way into leadership roles or positions, but rather being exposed to different environments and experiences. Seek out mentors that possess the necessary knowledge, skills, and clear understanding of your personal, professional, and academic areas of interest. This process is nothing new in most societies and business entities, but it is perceived by many to be too time consuming. As you seek your mentor, you will be surprised as to who would be willing to sacrifice their time to assist you in reaching all of your personal, professional, and academic goals.

THE IRREVERSIBLE CLOCK

"Lost time is never found again."

—Benjamin Franklin
Inventor, Writer, and Congressman

Time is the one resource that can never be replaced or replenished. Below is a passage about time by an unknown author that truly captures the essence of the value of time:

Imagine there is a bank that credits your account each morning with $86,400. It carries over no balance from day to day, allows you to keep no cash balance and, every evening, cancels whatever part of the amount you failed to use during the day. What would you do? Draw out every cent, of course. Well, everyone has such a bank. Its name is TIME. Every morning, it credits you with

86,400 seconds. Every night it writes off, as lost, whatever of this you have failed to invest to a good purpose. It carries over no balance, and it allows no overdraft. Each day it opens a new account for you. Each night it burns the records of the day. If you fail to use the day's deposits, the loss is yours. There is no going back. There is no drawing against the tomorrow. You must live in the present, on today's deposits. Invest it so as to get from it the utmost in health, happiness and success. The clock is running. Make the most of today.

To realize the value of one year:

Ask a student who has failed a final exam.

To realize the value of one month: Ask a mother who has given birth to a premature baby.

To realize the value of one week: Ask an editor of a weekly newspaper.

To realize the value of one hour: Ask lovers who are waiting to meet.

To realize the value of one minute: Ask someone who has missed a train, bus or plane.

To realize the value of one second: Ask someone who has survived an accident.

To realize the value of one millisecond: Ask someone who has won a silver medal in the Olympics.

Yesterday is history, tomorrow is a mystery, today is a gift, that's why it's called the present!

Treasure every moment that you have! And treasure it more because you shared it with someone special, special enough to have your time…and remember time waits for no one. Yesterday is a canceled check

Tomorrow is a promissory note

Today is cash on hand…spend it wisely!

Just as this excerpt shares, time is one of your most precious resources and an asset that should be guarded. As you develop your leadership ability, time becomes even more essential to this process. Do not waste it. Be careful to whom you give your time because you can never get it back.

The leadership development process takes time. Time is required to gain an education whether that education is formal or informal. Time is also required to gain meaningful or not so meaningful experiences. In order to comprehend and understand all that you have learned from your education and experiences takes time. Likewise, logic and common sense dictate that time is required to properly develop, teach, mentor, and coach future leaders who are capable of leading teams, groups, and organizations.

Through education, experience, and time, individuals who possess a sincere desire to lead others are capable of developing their leadership abilities. Of the three components mentioned, time is the only constant. Each of us is born with all the time that we will ever have or need in a lifetime. Leaders must focus on time management or rather "self-management," as you cannot manage time; for each of us only has 365 days per year, seven days per week, and 24 hours per day. There is no more; therefore, plan and use your time effectively, efficiently, and appropriately to achieve all the goals and objectives you have for yourself and your organization. Don't waste your time and don't allow others to waste your time. Time is the only resource available to a leader that can never be replenished.

EFFECTIVE COMMUNICATION

"Success for leadership is...knowing the great art of directing others without their noticing it."

—Unknown Author

Effective communication is essential to leadership. Leaders must be capable of communicating to their followers on many levels ranging from professional to personal aspects of a follower's life. There has to be a connection or a flow of communication between the leader and the follower in order for the leader to be effective. The ability to read minds is not a prerequisite to be a leader; nor is it a requirement to be a follower. However, the ability to effectively communicate is an essential component to leadership and it does not come easy. It requires that the leader have an understanding of the target audience

and what kindles their motivation. Through this understanding, a leader is better able to communicate with
their followers.

Effective communication is an art that must be developed and nurtured over time. Much like leadership, one's
ability to effectively communicate is contingent upon
education, experience, time, and a firm understanding
of what is being communicated. Without the ability to
know who you, as a leader, are communicating with, you
may be perceived as arrogant, condescending, or even as
a simpleton because you may be unclear as to what you
are communicating.

There are numerous means to communicate an individual's ideas (spoken word, written word, body language,
images, or a combination of all), but no one method is
better than another. Give them all a try. What do you
have to lose? Leaders must know who their target audience is and determine, based on this knowledge, the most
effective method in which to communicate with them.
One method that may have worked in the past may not
work in the future. A leader must constantly assess the
situation to find the right method to communicate with

to their followers. As the situation changes, your method of communicating must change as well.

Communication is a two-way street. Through effective communication, leaders communicate their intent, receive information, make important decisions and establish and foster relationships. It is your responsibility as a leader to learn how to communicate with everyone within your span of influence. Followers take leads from the leaders not vise-versa. The leader needs to be capable of communicating their message so clearly that followers, or anyone else they hope to influence in the process, can understand it. Remember this: in general, the followers you are trying to communicate with think, act, and process information differently than you do. This does not mean they are not intelligent, but rather they are not privy to the inner-workings of your vision. If you are perched up on your lofty stoop waiting for your followers to rise to your level of communication enlightenment, I am here to tell you that you will be waiting a long time for that to happen. If your followers don't know or understand what it is you, as a leader, want them to accomplish, chances are you won't get what you need from them.

Leaders, by virtue of their very nature, tend to be effective communicators. They have the ability to clearly communicate their vision and intentions to their followers, who are charged with carrying out the leader's vision and intentions. If they do not possess these abilities then they must identify this as a weakness and build upon it. As a leader, never underestimate the power of effective communication within your team, group, or organization.

TECHNOLOGY'S IMPACT

"Water is essential for soup — but soup is more than water. Competence is essential for business — but business is more than competence. What is added to water gives the 'value' of the soup. What is added to competence gives the value delivered by business. Competence is becoming a commodity. Information is becoming a commodity. State of the art technology is becoming a commodity. So what is going to differentiate businesses? How are these commodities to be designed to deliver value? That means design. That means creativity. That means new ideas. Ideas are going to become more important in business than they have ever been."

—Edward de Bono
U.S. leading authority in the field of human thinking and
Originator of Lateral Thinking

Leadership has undergone a transformation as a result of modern innovations in technology. Some of these changes have been beneficial to the leadership process, while others, as a whole, have been detrimental to effective leadership. The implementation of computers in all facets of business since the 1970s has effectively increased productivity and streamlined many tasks. Technology streamlines the processes of business by increasing efficiency in creating, analyzing, and printing (or otherwise transferring media) office work. The effective use of computer technology allows workers to create written documents faster and with more precision. Technology's impact extends from the reorganization of inventory accuracy and data analysis to improving presentation technology and overall quality of office presentations. In addition, fax machines and e-mail now allow for the transmittal of written documents instantly, computers track inventories and schedules, and word-processors ease the process of creating, correcting, and altering written work.

Technology is an asset to all organizations, but how does it affect leadership? Many times content gets lost along the path to perfection. Leaders fail to focus on the important aspects of the presentations and spend too much time concentrating on the presentation itself.

In other words, they become overly concerned about its flawlessness. The pursuit of this unattainable standard slows the wheels of business, for as leaders demand perfection in presentation and format there is too much emphasis placed on appearance, rather than content.

One of the most widely abused forms of technology by leaders is email. The overuse of email encourages leaders to avoid direct contact with employees in favor of email communication. While some leaders see email as beneficial in avoiding confrontation, distributing information quickly, or assigning unpleasant tasks, the use of email to accomplish leadership tasks makes less effective leaders, for they lose contact with their followers (employees). Additionally, inter-office communication via email, while saving paper, destroys formal writing within an organization, and produces loopholes through which accountability is lost concerning tasks, assignments, and protocols. Lastly, email contributes to another leadership detractor known as "information overload." Widespread dissemination of inapplicable information to lower levels of the organizational leadership overwhelms and detracts focus from the more important organizational issues.

The same can be said for office intranets and the Internet with respect to storing organizational data. There are literally billions of gigabytes of server storage out there for the purpose of information sharing within and outside of organizations. Any one organization could have thousands upon thousands of office documents stored in cyber space for use by its leaders and managers. Who has the time to sort through all this information to find the relevant information, much less the time to read and properly analyze it all? This phenomenon known as "information overload" has more or less backfired and resulted in leader inaction rather than action. The leader that is courtesy-copied dozens of large emails is more likely to electronically file the email with intent to review it later (but never actually doing so because of arrival of new emails he must pick through) or more easily hit the delete key and pretend he never saw it. Or how about the leader that is constantly told to review new regulations, policies, or other documents that are stored in a confusing and cumbersome company intranet. By the time the leader figures out which locations on the intranet to look in and which versions of the documents are most current he has wasted valuable time behind a desk when he could have been out front inspiring his followers.

Nevertheless, these technological tools can enhance your organization and supplement the leadership process if used effectively. Knowledge management is the key to providing exactly the information needed to the proper individuals without overwhelming them with extraneous information they do not require. This will allow today's leaders to minimize the time spent behind a desk and computer and get out in front of their followers where they belong.

When leaders regularly abuse these technologies, it is detrimental to the leadership process, thus yielding a change in office culture, the detachment of leaders from their followers, and ultimately blunting effective, concise communication in the workplace. Leadership is all about people and connecting with your followers. Remember, technology can enhance but cannot replace the human component in an organization.

EFFECTIVE LEADERSHIP

"Trust men and they will be true to you; treat them greatly, and they will show themselves great."

—Ralph Waldo Emerson
American Philosopher, Essayist, Poet &
Lecturer

The synergy of leadership is a powerful resource that can be used to achieve the goals and objectives of organizations. The leaders of an organization can send their followers into a frenzy with nothing more than a casual statement. This statement if construed incorrectly can cost an organization a great deal of money in man-hours wasted and expended resources. If persons begin moving in a direction that was not intended by the leader because they thought the leader wanted or expected something that the leader did not intend to convey, it can cause a great deal of disarray within an organization. A quote written by an unknown author was found hanging on the wall of a high school guidance counselor: "I believe you think you understand what I am saying, but I am not sure you realize what I said is not necessarily what I mean." Have you ever been in a meeting where a follower perceives that the leader would like for them to do something and everyone goes into a mad panic to make it happen, only to find out at a much later date that that was not what the leader had intended? This is the awesome power of leadership's influence at work.

Leaders need to be exceptionally aware of the influence they possess when interacting with their followers. Through effective leadership, leaders are better able to influence the actions of followers who have shared a common interest. Leadership is the process of consistently influencing other individuals toward the achievement of some goal or objective. It occurs throughout all levels of organizations and throughout societies. Absolutely nothing happens in organizations, institutions, and governments without some type of leadership being exercised by someone. It is the vision of the leader, if conveyed properly, that inspires and influences individuals to achieve the goals and objectives of the organization.

The key to truly effective leadership rests in mastering a wide range of skills, from implementing and administering processes to inspiring others to achieve excellence. Effective leaders make the most of opportunities in order to learn how to lead, whether by observing others, through formal education and training, or through careful evaluation of practical experience. These tasks provide a leader with a thorough grounding in essential skills and show how to put them into action in a variety of situations. Unfortunately, I have seen many so-called organizational leaders enact change simply for the sake of change in order to give others the impression that they are doing something, and in essence, earning their keep. Effective leadership of any organization must seek adaptive and constructive change only when necessary; they should never change for the sake of change.

Leaders must be capable of motivating, empowering, and creating initiative within their followers. They may help to achieve this by being consistent, for consistency yields predictability. Additionally, competency creates confidence, which increases morale and builds cohesion, making an organization more effective in completing its tasks. There are some leaders who believe so much in what it is that they are doing or trying to achieve that others around them perceive them to be passionate to a fault. Many leaders are so passionate about their vision that they apply valuable resources and great effort to achieve it. They become completely enmeshed in their vision and are driven to achieve it at much cost and sacrifice of personal time and motivation. Most leaders hope to instill this passion into their followers, for a leader's passion can truly be infectious.

Effective leaders must be capable of establishing relationships with their followers while maintaining a professional distance. Field Marshal Erwin Rommel stated, "The commander must try, above all, to establish personal and comradely contact with his men, but without giving away an inch of his authority." True leaders establish relationships, but they have the ability to separate themselves from the system and focus on the bigger picture.

BALANCING PERSONAL SACRIFICE
WITH COLLECTIVE RISK

"Throw away those books and cassettes on inspirational leadership. Send those consultants packing. Know your job, set a good example for the people under you and put results over politics. That's all the charisma you will ever need to succeed."

—Dyan Machan
Journalist and Senior Editor of Forbes Magazine

Yes, leadership requires sacrifice on part of the individual who wants to be a true leader. If it were an easy process, everyone would be doing it. There are many people within our society that do not want anything to do with leadership because it is perceived as too difficult, and that's okay, too. Leadership is not something that can be achieved overnight, by reading a book, or by taking a class. To develop your true leadership potential, you must make personal sacrifices, be disciplined, work hard, and be willing to assume risk in your attainment of it.

Individuals cannot be risk aversive in their pursuit of effective leadership. A simple way of looking at risk can be summed up with a quote that I once heard: "With great risk comes great reward!" Calculated risk is part of the leadership game. Leaders need to be capable of making timely decisions by quickly analyzing situations and determining the associated risk. They must be willing to stand by their convictions and do what they know is right for their followers and their organization, even if their decision is not a popular one at the moment.

President George W. Bush is an excellent example of a leader who is capable of standing by his convictions and decisions. Even though the President has received much criticism from his opponents, some American citizens, and other world leaders, he has stood steadfast on the issue of terrorism and the war in Iraq. He has accepted complete responsibility for what has happened or failed to happen with the war on terrorism and Operation Iraqi Freedom. Furthermore, President Bush did not waver or succumb to political correctness or to a personal desire to be re-elected into the office of Commander in Chief of the Armed services.

No one ever said leadership would be easy. Leaders understand that the past cannot be changed, so they don't dwell on it, but rather they learn from it. The present is happening right now, do what you can to effectively lead change today. But the future, on the other hand, has not yet been decided on. You must do what you can to properly position yourself, your followers, and your organization for the challenges you will be confronted with in the future. As a true leader, you can affect the future of your organization and the future of your followers through effective leadership practices.

You owe it to your followers to properly and effectively guide them today and in the future by applying effective leadership in all your leadership endeavors. In recent years, the ability to choose the harder right over the easier wrong has taken a back seat to political correctness and personal desires. Fear of being alienated, rebuffed, and even the loss of one's position has produced a society of spineless "yes men" who are willing to look the other way if there is personal gain in it for them. What good is a fancy title or promotion if you cannot look in the mirror and feel good about who you see looking back at you? Effective leaders will not take shortcuts to bring their vision to fruition. Through a leaders ability to influence their followers they can voluntarily move an organization towards set goals and objectives thereby achieving their critical purpose in an effective and efficient manner without compromising their integrity. Without this ability, so-called leaders are nothing more than organizational figureheads.

It has been my experience that many people within organizations tend to be clock-watching, time biding individuals whose only interest in the organization's success is their paycheck. Often leaders are the only individuals within an organization that seem to have any sense of urgency in meeting the organization's goals and objectives. This tendency is more wide spread within organizations than people in positions of authority think or want to believe. Ignoring this fact hinders most organizations from achieving their true goals and objectives.

Many people want to be leaders, but do not understand the burden of responsibility and sacrifice that comes with leadership. As a leader, you take on the problems of the organization. You are the confidant and motivator for the entire organization and this does not come without a cost. Being an effective leader takes time and takes a toll on anyone who should be fortunate enough to find themselves having the ability to influence others towards their vision or goal. Your future is determined by what you do today, not tomorrow!

WALKING THE TIGHTROPE:
CONFIDENCE VS. ARROGANCE

"Get over yourself; we [leaders] are here for the soldiers [followers]."

—Colonel Robert T. Burns
Director of Training and Doctrine, United
States Army Air Defense Artillery Center,
Fort Bliss, Texas

There is a thin line between confidence and arrogance. When leaders are competent, it is usually the result of their education and experiences that have been nurtured and developed over a period of time. They understand that they have not arrived at their current level of leadership and responsibility on their own. True leaders realize through constant self-reflection that they have indeed arrived at their current position in life because of their own efforts, personal sacrifices, and the efforts of others (mentors, friends, family, and followers).

When leaders believe in their abilities due to their firm comprehension of the technical and tactical requirements of a given situation, they will perform their duties and responsibilities with a level of enthusiasm that cannot be mistaken for anything else but confidence. On the other hand, there is no room for arrogance in the leadership process. Arrogance begets arrogance; an organization full of "INDIVIDUALS" will never reach or sustain any substantial level of success.

I have found that leaders who are blatantly arrogant do not tend to be as competent as they would like for you to believe. On the contrary, in many cases, the exact opposite is true. These arrogant individuals generally surround themselves with people who are genuinely talented but do not have the confidence, conviction, or realized experience to separate themselves from these arrogant leaders. In organizations with blatantly arrogant leaders, the true talent of the organization lays within the followers of these leaders. Leadership requires individuals to be confident in their abilities, but it does not require individuals to be arrogant. Confidence and competence are your benchmark–strive to have both. At all costs avoid becoming arrogant in the process of developing your leadership abilities. By becoming arrogant you will break down all that you've worked to achieve.

Another valuable quality of a leader is that of respect. Respect is a two-way street. Leaders must give respect in order to get respect. Leadership is not a one-way proposition. It is a fair exchange between leader and follower. If you, as a leader, expect respect from your followers, you must give them respect in return. One can never presume that they are a leader if they do not have the respect and trust of their followers.

Arrogance hampers organizations from achieving their true potential. Followers choose to follow their leaders for many reasons. Therefore, leaders need to be more aware of the motivations (wants and needs) of their followers; it starts by being respectful of others. Get over yourself–there is no "I" in TEAM!

TYRANNICAL TREATMENT

"You do not lead by hitting people over the head–that's assault, not leadership."

—Dwight D. Eisenhower
34th President of the United States and
General, United States Army

Sadly, there are leaders who abuse their power and position. Tyrannical treatment undermines the effectiveness of an organization. To achieve results the tyrant must always be riding their followers, for once he is physically absent, minimal effort will be put forth and little work will get done. Followers will only produce results when the so-called leader is there to oversee what is taking place at that particular moment in time.

Tyrants also tend to be micromanagers. Do not be the leader that micromanages their followers. This is a style of management not of leadership. Micromanagement only brings down the already sagging morale in most organizations.

Leaders believe in people, seize the opportunity, and make things happen! I cannot state strongly enough that leadership is given to leaders by their followers. Influence is not coercion or harsh or tyrannical treatment of your followers. Actually, it is the opposite. Influence is a result of effective leadership. Without the ability to consistently influence other individuals without relying on fear, true leadership does not exist. Remember this as you read Major General John M. Schofield's address to the Corps of Cadets [United States Military Academy] on August 11, 1879.

[The] discipline which makes the soldiers of a free country reliable in battle is not to be gained by harsh or tyrannical treatment. On the contrary, such treatment is far more likely to destroy than to make an army. It is possible to impart instruction and to give commands in such a manner and such a tone of voice to inspire in the soldier no feeling but an intense desire to obey, while the opposite manner and tone of voice cannot fail to excite strong resentment and a desire to disobey. The one mode or the other of dealing with subordinates springs from a corresponding spirit in the breast of the commander. He who feels the respect which is due to others cannot fail to inspire in them regard for himself, while he who feels, and hence manifests, disrespect toward others, especially his inferiors, cannot fail to inspire hatred against himself.

True leaders are not tyrants. Through consistency of action, leaders inspire, motivate and influence their followers to achieve the goals and objectives of their organizations.

PROVIDING VISION

"I am more afraid of an army of 100 sheep led by a lion than an army of 100 lions led by a sheep."

—Charles Maurice de Talleyrand-Périgord Napoleon's grand chamberlain, Louis XVIII's Foreign Affairs Minister

With nothing more than a simple vision you can change yourself and the world. The ability of a leader to clearly visualize the infinite possibility of what they want to do and how to achieve it, is nothing short of extraordinary. The ability to see something that has not been conceived, created, or initiated is indeed a very powerful and special gift. One thing that sets leaders apart from other individuals is this ability to visualize what can be possible. Vision is a mental image produced by the imagination.

Leaders have vision. It is the vision of the leader that provides the purpose for individuals and organizations to move forward even in the face of adversity. The leader's vision also establishes a road map (direction) of sorts for members within organizations to follow. This vision serves as a blue print for the organization that can be modified as the need arises to ensure that the goals and objectives of the organization are achieved.

Vision requires leaders to have imagination, understand the relevance of what is to be accomplished, and the ability to critically think through the endless possibilities that may affect the outcome of their vision. This is not to say that the leader's vision is somehow supernatural in nature, but rather it is the leader's ability to think holistically about what their teams, groups, and organizations have to accomplish in the short, near, and most importantly, the long-term to achieve success.

It is the leader's vision or ability to visualize things that do not yet exist that makes them different from their followers. The leader's vision must be effectively communicated to everyone in the organization if it is to ever be fully realized. Visions should be articulated as a written statement to help effectively communicate a clear and concise understanding of the long-term goals and objectives underlying the leader's vision. The most effective way I have been able to convey my vision has been through what I refer to as the leader's intent statement. It is made up of three parts: the purpose, the key(s) points to success, and the organizational end state.

Over the years, I have modified this leader's intent statement from the United States Army Commander's Intent format. The leader's intent statement is brief in nature but very comprehendible. The leader's intent will clearly state to your target audience the purpose of the required actions to be completed. Be sure that the purpose that you are communicating ties back to the organization's goal(s), objective(s), or mission statement.

Immediately following the purpose statement are the key points to success, which are captured in a concise bullet format. They identify critical tasks that must be accomplished in order to achieve this particular purpose. The key(s) points to success also focus the follower on the important issues, while allowing them the initiative to be creative in their efforts to make the leader's vision a reality.

The key(s) points to success are followed by the organizational end state that is expected of the required actions to be completed. This end state is nothing more than a brief statement of how the leader envisions his organization at the end of the completed actions. Everyone in an organization must be able to extract the leader's intent in order to meet the expectations of the leader's vision. Provided below is an example of a leader's intent in the described format:

Purpose:

The purpose of Lifestream Technologies (LFTC) is to bring innovative medical diagnostic products to the professional market. All of our products are designed to be affordable while providing quick measurement of total cholesterol to aid in disease prevention, diagnosis, and control.

Key(s) Points to Success:

1 Develop the first home cholesterol monitor incorporating an embedded smart card reader

2 Be the leading manufacturer of smart card-enabled healthcare diagnostic devices

3 Receive FDA clearance for cholesterol monitors for healthcare professionals and consumers

4 Increase shareholder value

Organizational End State:

The end state for this venture are satisfied customers who can check their cholesterol anywhere and at anytime; to become the chosen cholesterol monitoring devices in two out of three homes in America capable of providing customers with accurate, fast, and simple test readings; and to increase shareholder value.

By using the leader's intent statement, leaders can disseminate concise and relevant information to their followers. Delivering the information (vision) in this format provides the follower with a clear purpose, while informing them why their actions are important to the success of the team, group, or organization. The leader's intent statement also focuses the followers on all of the key points that must be accomplished for the organization to be successful at a particular undertaking. This allows the follower the opportunity to apply their initiative in completing various tasks in order to meet the goals and objectives of the organization. If the purpose has been met through the successful completion of all key points then the organizational end state will be realized. The leader's intent statement is nothing more than a tool that can be used by the leader to focus the effort of their followers in achieving the goals and objectives of the organization while realizing the vision of the leader.

As a leader you must get your followers involved in your vision. Ensure they know why they are doing the things that they do for your organization, and they will be more inclined to make your vision into a reality. Treat your followers like the precious resource that they are. Your organization needs followers just as it needs leaders. Think about it!

INTANGIBLE PROCESS – QUANTIFIABLE PRODUCT

"The leader has to be practical and a realist, yet must talk the language of the visionary and the idealist."

—Eric Hoffer
Author, Philosopher, and Experienced
Longshoreman

Leadership is not a tangible characteristic. You cannot touch it, smell it or see it, but it can be *quantified* through the success an organization achieves or through the success an individual achieves in their personal, professional, and academic lives. The future has not been written, but the actions that you take today will determine how your future turns out tomorrow.

True leadership is a highly sought after and valuable *quality* that many organizations are willing to pay handsomely to acquire. Many CEOs receive salaries in the millions, not to mention the additional millions they receive in stock options and bonuses. These leaders, through their academic discipline and vast experiences within their chosen field or profession, are able to harness the leadership qualities that enable them to succeed in their personal, professional, and academic endeavors.

Over the course of my lifetime I have been privy to witness many different styles of leadership utilized to achieve the goals and objectives of organizations. Some of these leadership styles were worthy of further scrutiny, while others were better left unrealized.

Leadership is the fuel that enables organizations to succeed within any industry or realm. On the other hand, a lack of leadership surely aids in the failure of individuals and organizations. I am sure that there are a few people who still do not believe that leadership is a *tangible ingredient* in the success of an organization, but true leadership is, in fact, the cornerstone of any successful organization. It is the leadership of an organization that determines the direction that organization takes in its pursuit of goals and objective obtainment. This leadership also determines how quickly an organization will arrive at its goal and ensures the organization functions in the manner for which it was intended. If the leader of any organization, regardless of how big or small, fails to effectively communicate their intent to their followers, the effect will be a splintered organization that lacks synchronization and is overall ineffective.

Leadership is about people, human dynamics, and how individuals interact within their environment and one another. Leadership is the ultimate people game that can be quantified by the consistent results achieved (organizational goals and objectives) by teams, groups and organizations.

TOMORROW'S LEADERS

"Men make history, and not the other way around. In periods where there is no leadership, society stands still. Progress occurs when courageous, skillful leaders seize the opportunity to change things for the better."

—Harry S. Truman
33rd U.S. President, Established NATO

The development of future leaders within organizations must be the top priority of any organization. In a number of instances, the development of future leaders is something that is glazed over, or worse yet, the thought never occurs to anyone to develop future leaders needed to continue leading their organization. In these cases, developing leaders is an after thought rather than a priority. The need for leaders within any institution, society, or government will never disappear or be replaced by anything, not even technology.

The ability to create a vision, think critically, and make sound decisions is something that can only be achieved by living, breathing, and conscious human beings. These traits are so valuable that to think of leadership as an afterthought is preposterous. To seek leadership at a time of need, rather than anticipating and developing the leaders needed to sustain the growth and integrity of an organization in the future, will lead to bad decisions that are hastily implemented and poorly executed. In addition, this reactionary method will create an organization destined for ultimate failure.

We, as a society, have become what I affectionately refer to as a "shake and bake society" that wants, not needs, everything right now. This is acceptable for microwave products but does not fit into the true leadership development process. The leadership process takes time and involves a great commitment on the part of all involved.

Developing the leadership potential within future leaders cannot and should not be a painful process. Leadership development as a process, if done correctly over a period of time, can produce future leaders that are competent and capable of assuming a myriad of dynamic roles within any organization. The development of leaders that are capable of assuming challenging and difficult positions within organizations requires a commitment of time, opportunity, and resources. Current organizational leaders are obligated by virtue of their authority and position to commit these necessary ingredients as well as committing the time to teach, coach, and mentor their followers.

Leaders must approach the leadership development process from the standpoint that future leaders only know what they know. Leaders cannot assume that their followers or future leaders have gained all of the education and experiences that are required to lead teams, groups, and organizations to success through academic and training means alone. This is surely a recipe for failure.

As a leader you can't just assume that you have the right fit between follower and position and/or task(s). This is common sense, but as I have come to realize over the years, common sense is not so common. In keeping with what I know to be true, individuals are the sum total of all of their experiences, and they only know what they know. Therefore, if an individual has not been exposed to and has not had the opportunity or experience of a particular situation, there is no possible way that the individual can conceptualize and internalize the complexities of a situation, unless they can think critically about a given situation.

All leaders must ensure they foster and maintain a positive learning environment that facilitates creative thinking or the ability to think outside of the box. These strategic thinkers help to further the organization's goals and objectives. Having followers who follow you blindly does not facilitate the success of the organization; for when the leader is no longer present, they will have no ability to take the initiative and lead when they are needed. Followers who have not "bought in" to the vision of the leader will not utilize their initiative or hone their leadership abilities. This is where mentorship becomes essential.

Mentorship has a special place in the development of leadership. This is true regardless of the organization type or size. There are many of you that would dismiss mentorship as a waste of time. Given the current state of affairs in many organizations today, I would disagree. Mentorship is not a fly by night fad or a buzzword that many organizations have adopted in an attempt to show a softer or more understanding side of leadership in power at a particular time.

There are many of you who would be suspect if your boss or supervisor showed you any additional attention. Some of you would be correct in this assumption and suspicion, while others would be incorrect. I always say, "Be suspect of all that stand before you." This is not a pessimistic statement. It simply means that you should not assume that everyone has your best interest in mind. I feel that it is better to be cautious and have your eyes wide open to determine what lays ahead in an effort to make more informed decisions about to whom you give your trust, respect, admiration, and most importantly, to whom you give your time. However, for leaders, spending extra time to mentor followers is essential.

I have seen and identified the potential in many followers over the years and have mentored those individuals in an effort to ensure that they would achieve a level of success that would otherwise go unnoticed or untapped without intervention. By engaging in mentorship you have nothing to lose. On the other hand, you stand to gain a valuable resource that can make your position and life richer and more enjoyable.

MORGAN'S TIPS FOR SUCCESS

Some points to keep succeeding in your leading

- Loyalty is a two-way street
- First seek to understand, and then do
- Think outside of the box – forego the status quo
- Awareness and understanding leave little room for conflict
- Be approachable
- Prepare followers to be proficient in their jobs
- Trust your followers and they will trust you in return
- Delegate to followers if they are competent
- If you ignore the minimum standard, you set a new standard (a lower one)
- Remain enthusiastic

- Remain realistic in establishing your goals and objectives
- Not everything is a crisis or an emergency
- Everyday you make a decision to be what you are – a leader or a follower
- When in charge, take charge
- Keep your followers informed and they will keep you informed
- Leaders must know how to follow, if they ever hope to lead
- Stay in your lane and demand that others remain in their lane

Keep your finger on the pulse of your organization

WHAT DO YOU DO NOW?

"It is not the technical skills, hard knowledge or intelligence that makes fast track selling professionals effective in their jobs. Most of the time, it is their superior skill in handling people that propels their career, boosts productivity and ensures their job satisfaction."

—Dan Brent Burt
U.S. IBM acct. manager and sales director,
popular lecturer and author

Cracking the Nut on Leadership was written not as a how-to manual or as a stand-alone source, but rather to bring about more awareness to the topic of leadership. Now that the nut has been cracked, it is my sincere desire to have you take this new level of consciousness about the vital role leadership plays in all of our lives so that you may gather more information about this very powerful topic.

Through the information presented you should find yourself thinking about leadership in a different capacity and be better prepared and further along in the educational process needed to make you a more effective leader.

Leadership is a developmental process, which can be learned and improved upon. It first begins with an awareness of yourself and your environment. This includes having a firm understanding of how you as an individual are affected by your surroundings as well as how you affect all those things outside of yourself. Once you have this awareness, you can begin to figure out how you need to approach your situation. Therefore, you must possess a firm understanding of your fit into the larger context of what you do and why you do it. For instance, if you look at most of your followers to be inherently lazy and only concerned with themselves, you will more than likely micromanage; you won't delegate and you will generally tend to be condescending and judgmental towards them. On the other hand, if you approach leadership believing that most followers want to do a good job and be part of a team, you will have a more laissez-faire attitude towards leadership; you will delegate more and tend to trust your followers.

No one leadership approach will be effective in all situations. You must be aware of the benefits and limitations in your approach. This is just one of the many aspects of leadership which leads to its complexity. Leadership requires much effort to develop the ability to analyze different situations and consistently arrive at solutions that meet the goals and objectives of teams, groups, and organizations. This is not to say that leaders always make the right decision, but it is to say that more often than not leaders are capable of making sound decisions. Leadership is about choices.

Regardless of how much effort was placed into a decision, it does not negate the fact that a decision was made. Remember that even doing nothing at all requires a decision to be made. I would advocate that you be an active participant in everything that impacts you and the world that you are a part of. We all in hindsight realize that there are certain actions that we should have taken, as well as situations where we should have acted and we did not. We cannot relive the decisions that were made;

however, we can learn from our shortcomings, failures, and successes.

Leadership mandates that a true leader be a lifelong learner, open to new ideas, be trustworthy, respectful of others, and possess the personal courage to stand by their convictions even if others do not agree. In order to gain the education and the experiences needed to develop your leadership potential, you must be willing to take risks. Individuals who are afraid of failing tend to succumb to mediocrity and the status quo. This will never afford you the freedom of being a true leader who is capable of changing the direction of individuals, teams, groups, organizations and the world. Leaders must be capable of consistently demonstrating the personal courage to do what is right for the organization and its individuals even if others do not agree with them. This is why they are leaders and not followers. If it were easy, everyone would be a leader.

If you cannot consistently influence the actions of others, you are not a leader. It seems to me that people follow leaders for a variety of reasons. Some because they look up to you and respect you, others because they follow out of fear of being left behind, and some out of simple curiosity. Why they follow you does not matter, what matters is your ability as a leader to be able to consistently influence them in such a manner that they want to continue to follow you.

Leadership transcends all boundaries, classes, and social structures. If there is a group or organization, there will always be leadership present within these social structures. The bottom line on leadership is it requires an individual to possess the ability to consistently influence the actions of others. Leadership is not a popularity contest, although it would seem as though this is the case when you examine the processes utilized to choose leaders within many organizations today. True leadership is about results. Organizations live and die by their leadership; their success or failure is dependant upon it.

My understanding of the game is quite simple. He who has more options wins in the end. Feel free to quote me on this! What I truly care about is an awareness regarding the subject of leadership and how leadership impacts (positive or negative) everything and everyone on this planet. The system is not designed to take care of everyone. The system is designed to take care of those that are part of this stream of consciousness and know enough to understand that they are, in fact, part of a system, something larger than themselves.

I stand by my statement that you only know what you know. Therefore, it should go without saying that if people were more aware of what leadership is and is not and what it means to be a leader, they would become more involved within their community to ensure competent and committed individuals were being selected as leaders to make the decisions that impact their families, communities, and the world. Effective leadership should not be the exception, but rather the rule. Therefore, our leaders need to know that we are watching. When will we be watching you?

ABOUT THE AUTHOR

Written by Keith W. DeGregory
Captain, U.S. Army

Years ago I had the great privilege of serving under Samuel Morgan. Samuel was able to bring out the best in me and inspired me to reach my true leadership potential; he made me realize things about myself which would have went untapped without his active involvement and true concern for my development as a leader.

When Samuel first told me he was writing this book I was skeptical because I had no idea how he would be able to fit it into his already packed schedule. Not only was he finishing up a 20 year military career as an Army Officer at the time, but he also had established his own photography business, 20/20 Imaging; co-founded a leadership consulting firm, RowlandMorgan Group, LLC; he was serving as an adjunct professor teaching Management and Organizational Leadership at Webster University; and all along was pursuing a Doctorate of Philosophy in leadership.

Samuel has an astonishing knack for taking on the world and being successful at everything he embarks on. This is due greatly to his deep passion for the function that leadership plays in life and organizations.

His background with leadership started when he enlisted in the U.S. Military in 1984. As a Special Forces (Green Beret) soldier Samuel was able to truly understand leadership from the other side by being on the receiving end of orders and commands. Samuel was later commissioned as an Infantry Officer and went on to lead an Infantry Company of more than 120 soldiers. Appropriately, one of Samuel's last positions in the military was instructing career military officers, both U.S. and U.S. Allied Nations, and preparing them for the great responsibilities of leading American and Allied soldiers as future company commanders.

His qualifications are endless and include some of

the best training that the military and U.S. educational institutions have to offer. He has received leadership training from the vast military schools he has graduated from to include: Special Forces, Airborne, Ranger, Air Assault, SERE (Survive, Evade, Resist, and Escape), Freefall Parachutist, Small Group Instructor Training Course, and foreign language training. As for his civilian education he holds a B.S. in Management and Business Administration, a M.A. in Management, and is currently a doctoral candidate in Philosophy in Organizational Behavior with emphasis in Leadership.

If you are not yet convinced by his educational background and practical experience with leadership then take the word from one who has truly been inspired by his passion. Samuel wants nothing more than to share his knowledge and experience with as many as he can in hopes of making better leaders that run our private businesses and government. With as many books on leadership available at the bookstores as there are styles of leadership; it is important that the reader of this book understand that Samuel merely provides "a way" to help people apply effective leadership. Short of receiving

Samuel's extraordinary mentorship first hand as I did, the next best thing is to read this book.

ISBN 1-41205146-0

9 781412 051460